THE 10™

Most Extraordinary Medical Conditions

Barbara Winter

Series Editor
Jeffrey D. Wilhelm

Much thought, debate, and research went into choosing and ranking the 10 items in each book in this series. We realize that everyone has his or her own opinion of what is most significant, revolutionary, amazing, deadly, and so on. As you read, you may agree with our choices, or you may be surprised — and that's the way it should be!

an imprint of

■SCHOLASTIC

www.scholastic.com/librarypublishing

A Rubicon book published in association with Scholastic Inc.

Ru'bicon © 2007 Rubicon Publishing Inc.
www.rubiconpublishing.com

Associate Publishers: Kim Koh, Miriam Bardswich
Project Editor: Amy Land
Editor: Joyce Thian
Creative Director: Jennifer Drew
Project Manager: Jeanette MacLean
Graphic Designers: Deanna Bishop, Victoria Cigan
Editorial Consultant: Andrew Alexis, MD, MPH

The publisher gratefully acknowledges the following for permission to reprint copyrighted material in this book.

Every reasonable effort has been made to trace the owners of copyrighted material and to make due acknowledgment. Any errors or omissions drawn to our attention will be gladly rectified in future editions.

"Beyond the Limbs, a Disease's Hidden Agony" (excerpt) by Donald G. McNeil Jr. from *The New York Times*, April 9, 2006. Copyright © 2006 by The New York Times Co. Reprinted with permission.

"'Bubble boy comes home from hospital" (excerpt) by Elaine Carey. From the *Toronto Star*, June 3, 2006. Reprinted with permission from Torstar Syndication Services.

Cover: Skeleton X-ray–Getty Images/Digital Vision/dv385010

Library and Archives Canada Cataloguing in Publication

Winter, Barbara
   The 10 most extraordinary medical conditions / Barbara Winter.

Includes index.
ISBN 978-1-55448-481-2

   1. Readers (Elementary) 2. Readers—Diseases. I. Title. II. Title: Ten most extraordinary medical conditions.

PE1117.W5425 2007a   428.6   C2007-901987-0

1 2 3 4 5 6 7 8 9 10   10   16 15 14 13 12 11 10 09 08 07

Printed in Singapore

Contents

6

18

38

STRANGE BUT TRUE

You've probably had your share of coughs and colds, fevers and flus. No big deal, they're pretty ordinary, right? But, can you imagine coming down with something so unusual that even your doctor is stumped, shocked, and unable to help?

Even the brightest medical minds say there are medical conditions so different and unusual, they defy logic and comprehension. They're nothing like anything we know or understand as "normal."

The most extraordinary conditions stand out from the rest. The ones in this book are rare, cause bizarre and shocking symptoms, and have unexplainable causes. Doctors have great difficulty diagnosing and treating these conditions, some of which can even be fatal. When all these factors come together, even the medical world may not be able to cure or explain these extreme medical conditions!

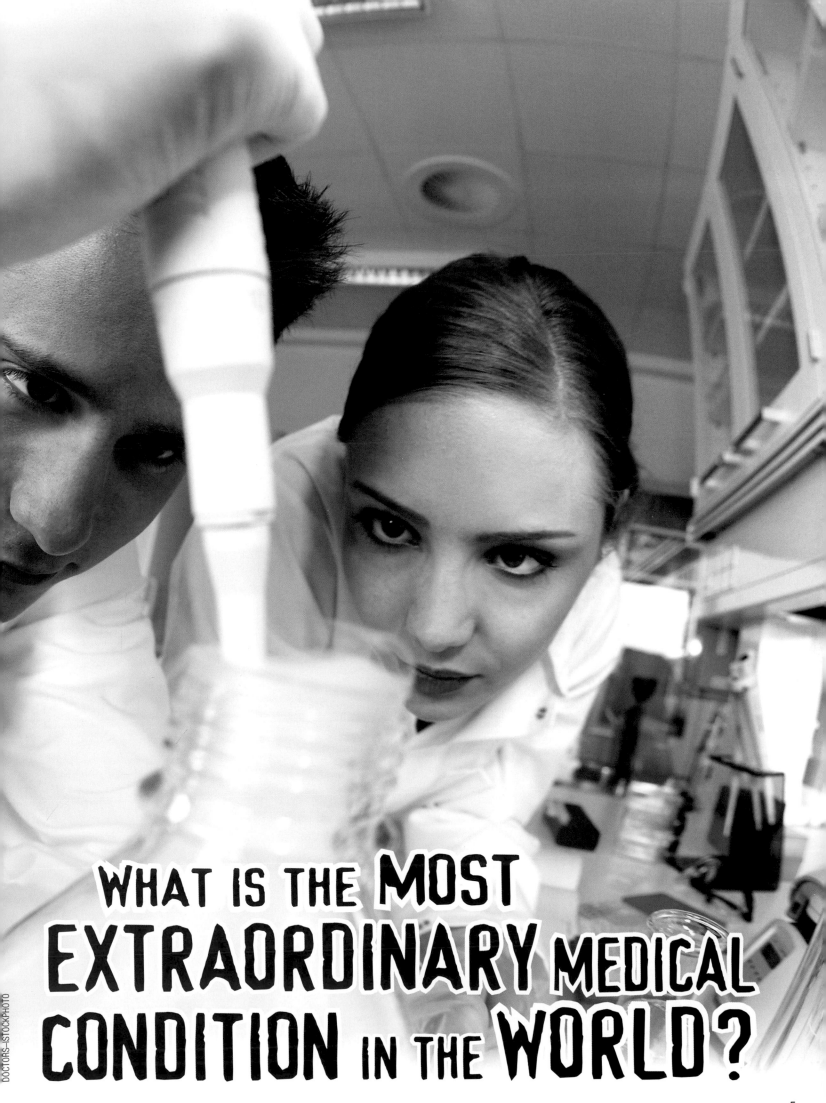

WHAT IS THE MOST EXTRAORDINARY MEDICAL CONDITION IN THE WORLD?

The majority of AIW sufferers are young children between the ages of five and 10.

NDERLAND

MEDICAL NAME: Alice in Wonderland syndrome, also known as AIW

CAUSE: Unknown

WHAT'S WRONG: The mind tricks the patient into thinking that objects and body parts appear to change shapes and sizes.

Alice in Wonderland (AIW) syndrome is named after the famous children's book in which Alice, the heroine, falls down a rabbit hole. She has fantastic adventures where she shrinks to a tiny size, or grows as big as a house. But there is nothing imaginary or fun about this condition, which causes patients to have strange visions similar to those in the book.

People with this disorder are perfectly normal — until they have an AIW episode. One minute they're feeling fine and the next, they can only watch in shock as their arm or their leg suddenly grows into a gigantic version of itself …

AIW has puzzled doctors for over 50 years. Clearly, limbs cannot change in size. Are these patients just imagining all the stretching (and shrinking) that they see every now and then? And what's a doctor supposed to think if brain scans and eye exams all come back normal?

Read on to find out more about this extraordinary medical condition and see if you can figure out the mystery.

CAUSE

People with AIW have been tricked by their own brains! The illusions that AIW patients "see" are the result of the brain misreading messages sent by the eyes. Doctors still don't know exactly what's going on in the brain when this happens. Even brain scans haven't helped much in the way of discovering the mystery behind AIW.

? Have you ever heard someone say, "I won't believe it till I see it with my very own eyes"? Experts who have studied AIW may disagree with this saying. Why would that be?

SYMPTOMS

The symptoms of AIW vary from person to person. Most patients feel as if their body or its parts are either shrinking or stretching. Some patients get the feeling that objects around them have suddenly become very small and far away or extremely large and close. During these episodes, it's hard to do even ordinary tasks like walking straight. Some people with AIW have trouble speaking or feel like they're dreaming or in a trance.

TREATMENT

Because doctors don't know what causes AIW, they cannot treat people with this problem. Sometimes, AIW vanishes by itself (or maybe it just seems like it, because people get tired of telling doctors over and over again about visions that can't be explained). Because most people who have AIW also have migraines, some believe that avoiding certain foods that cause migraine attacks can also help control AIW symptoms.

migraines: *very bad headaches*

The Expert Says...

" Patients with these symptoms may understandably fear for their sanity. "

— Stewart Cameron in *Medical Post*

10   9   8   7   6

Here is a medical report of a female patient growing up with AIW:

PATIENT NAME	Doe, Ms. Jane	SEX	REFERRING DOCTOR	GHT
REF. No:	65/G298 DATE 05.12.06	M ☐ F ☑	REPORT: Patient has a history of migraines.	

DESCRIPTION OF EPISODES:

• First episode took place when patient was just 10 years old. Patient says she woke up one morning and felt like she was still asleep and dreaming. When she held out her hands in front of her, they didn't feel like her hands. They were like long and skinny twigs. This feeling went away after a few minutes, so she did not report it to her parents.

• More episodes similar to the above happened repeatedly, usually at night.

• Patient notes that if she is sitting during an episode, she starts feeling incredibly heavy, so much so that she becomes unsure of whether she can move any part of her body.

• Patient says that once, while she was walking down a hall, she felt like the walls were suddenly rushing past her at very high speeds.

• Another episode occurred one afternoon after patient got home from school. She was sitting on her bed when she noticed that a part of the headboard started to move and spin like a wheel.

• These recurring episodes make patient feel frustrated. She says she knows that her body and these objects aren't actually doing these things, but her brain is telling her that they are.

• Every episode is accompanied with a strange feeling like extreme light-headedness, as if patient is on laughing gas.

Take Note

We included Alice in Wonderland syndrome in the book because doctors are still unable to explain its mysterious symptoms. But compared to the other medical conditions in this book, it is far less dangerous and deadly. That is why we have placed it at #10.
• What are the difficulties patients may have with a condition that has no physical symptoms and cannot be explained?

9 ALIEN HAND

Patients with AHS can still feel sensation in their alien hand, but can no longer control its movements.

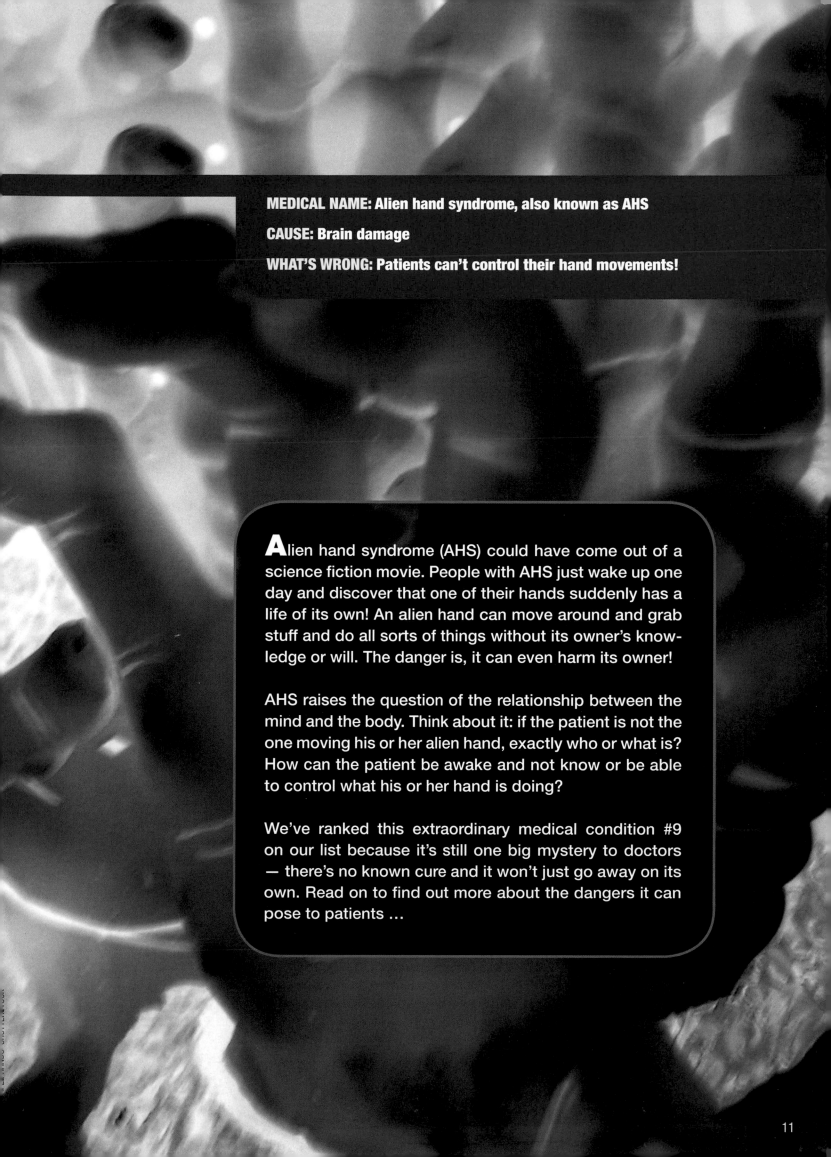

MEDICAL NAME: Alien hand syndrome, also known as AHS

CAUSE: Brain damage

WHAT'S WRONG: Patients can't control their hand movements!

Alien hand syndrome (AHS) could have come out of a science fiction movie. People with AHS just wake up one day and discover that one of their hands suddenly has a life of its own! An alien hand can move around and grab stuff and do all sorts of things without its owner's knowledge or will. The danger is, it can even harm its owner!

AHS raises the question of the relationship between the mind and the body. Think about it: if the patient is not the one moving his or her alien hand, exactly who or what is? How can the patient be awake and not know or be able to control what his or her hand is doing?

We've ranked this extraordinary medical condition #9 on our list because it's still one big mystery to doctors — there's no known cure and it won't just go away on its own. Read on to find out more about the dangers it can pose to patients …

ALIEN HAND

CAUSE

Because the brain is in charge of all body movements, any damage to a part of the brain can potentially lead to AHS. People who have had strokes, brain infections, and sometimes even botched brain surgeries, can fall victim to alien hand syndrome.

SYMPTOMS

The alien hand is capable of all kinds of different movements; it all depends on which part of the brain was damaged. An injury to the brain tissue that connects the two halves of the brain would make your non-dominant hand the alien one. An injury to the front section of the brain would give you an alien hand that grabs and jabs. More serious injuries (such as brain tumors or strokes) would result in alien hands that can do complex hand movements.

TREATMENT

For now, there's no known cure for AHS, because doctors haven't figured out how to repair the brain damage that causes it. Some people with AHS have at least discovered how to prevent their alien hand from intruding on their daily lives — by keeping it occupied! For example, a patient whose alien hand was always trying to touch things while he was walking gave his hand a cane to hold.

non-dominant hand: *hand you use less*

What other alien behaviors could result from brain damage? Hint: Our brains are in charge of much more than just hand movements!

The Expert Says...

"[Patients with AHS] may struggle to stop the movements, restrain the limb, punish it, talk to it, personify or refer to it as a third person. They may even say that an evil spirit exists in the hand."

— Dr. R. Inzelberg, neurologist, Hillel Yaffe Medical Center

10   **9**   8   7   6

Real-Life STORIES
FROM PEOPLE LIVING WITH AHS

Just how difficult can alien hands get?
Check out these short descriptive accounts!

A male patient would button his shirt with his good hand and then find his alien hand trying to unbutton it.

A 67-year-old man's hand crept and crawled, especially at night. Sometimes his hand would even wake him up by pulling at his shirt collar. How did doctors fix this night terror? By placing the man's hand in an oven mitt!

Two female patients thought of their hands as their children. One called it her "baby," and another named it "baby Joseph."

One patient complained that his left arm felt like a strange limb lying beside him. He said he hated his left arm, calling it a "jerk."

A patient was driving when he found himself in trouble at an intersection. His right hand wanted to turn left, but his left wanted to turn right!

A woman fell asleep and woke up one night finding someone choking her ... it was her own left hand! She managed to fight herself off with her right hand, but what a close call that was!

When asked to place a toothbrush in front of the mirror, a patient took the toothbrush with her right hand, but then her left hand snatched it and put it back where it was.

What other daily activities might become dangerous if you had something like AHS?

Take Note

Both #9 alien hand syndrome and #10 Alice in Wonderland syndrome are caused by brain disorders. But we ranked AHS higher than AIW because AHS can potentially cause serious harm to the patient.

- Some people call AHS "anarchic (chaotic) hand syndrome." Do you think this is a more appropriate name? Why or why not?

5   4   3   2   1

8 ST. ANTHONY'S

If left untreated, victims of ergot poisoning have been known to twist and twitch even when constrained to a bed.

FIRE

MEDICAL NAME: Ergotism (ur-get-tism), also known as St. Anthony's Fire

CAUSE: Food poisoning

WHAT'S WRONG: A fungus infection can make a patient feel as if his or her skin is on fire.

Ergotism is food poisoning to the extreme. It is caused by a fungus called ergot, which can grow in grains like rye and barley. Since ergot fungus grows best in damp conditions, ergot poisoning is most likely to occur after a long winter or a rainy spring.

Ergotism was a widespread problem in the past because back then, people weren't so careful when preparing grain. They often didn't check contaminated grain for ergot before turning it into flour, which would then be made into bread and cereal for the entire village, resulting in mass ergot poisoning.

Ergotism is sometimes called "St. Anthony's Fire." It makes sufferers feel like their skin is on fire. Before doctors found out what caused this disease or how to cure it, victims often lost limbs and even suffered brain damage!

The puzzling thing about this extraordinary condition is that the ergot fungus can actually be used to cure other ailments. For example, it can help manage migraines and prevent bleeding during childbirth.

ST. ANTHONY'S FIRE

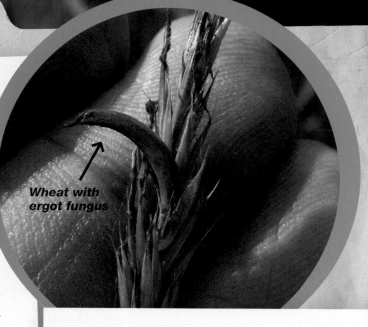

Wheat with ergot fungus

CAUSE

Poisoning from food contaminated by the ergot fungus.

SYMPTOMS

People who fall ill with ergotism usually start with a variety of symptoms: headaches and diarrhea, itching and twitching, nausea and vomiting. Parts of the body, such as fingers and toes, arms and legs, may start tingling. Then patients may get seizures and hallucinations. While all this is happening, the tingling starts turning into a burning sensation. The pain may get a lot worse because gangrene sets in soon after this. That's when the blood supply to the affected parts of the body is cut off. Without blood, body tissues begin to die, turning dry and black. Limbs start dropping right off — dead limbs are a very real part of this strange disease.

seizures: *sudden attacks, resulting in extreme muscle twitching*

hallucinations: *seeing things that aren't actually there*

TREATMENT

Back in the day when there were major outbreaks of ergot poisoning, nobody knew the cure for this strange disease. The only thing that seemed to help was keeping people who were sick in hospitals. Once they were in a hospital, they stopped eating their contaminated grain or bread from home.

Quick Fact

Some historians and scientists think that the "Witches of Salem" may have been victims of ergotism. They say the strange behavior that these women were charged with may have just been symptoms of ergot poisoning.

? What simple steps could people in the past have taken to prevent ergotism?

The Expert Says...

" A great plague of swollen blisters consumed the people by a loathsome rot, so that their limbs were loosened and fell off before death. "

— Earliest reference to ergotism from a medical book in the year 857

0 9 **8** 7 6

TOWN GONE MAD

This **article** describes one of the deadliest modern-day outbreaks of ergot poisoning.

On August 12, 1954, two patients went to see Dr. John Vieu. He thought their stomach pains might be appendicitis, except their body temperatures were too low. They said they felt cold even though it was a warm summer day. The next day, another patient came in with the same symptoms. When Dr. Vieu met with the town's other doctors, they found they had 20 patients between them, all with the same symptoms.

By August 14th, the hospital was full of sick people. Seventy houses were used as extra wards. A total of 230 people had become ill.

The sick all complained of feeling light-headed before they were struck with pain, vomiting, giddiness, and diarrhea. Some patients experienced hallucinations or depression; others became delirious, went into convulsions, or grew extremely agitated. Some people had to be tied to their beds — straitjackets were brought into the town to restrain the most violent. A dog that had also eaten contaminated bread ran around in wild circles, vomiting, until it collapsed and died.

In the end, four people died and 32 had brain damage in some degree. Those who survived said they couldn't forget the horrible burning sensations in their arms and legs — it felt as though insects were crawling under their skin. Some saw visions of weird deformed animals and fire and blood on the walls.

All in all, it was an experience that the survivors would always remember.

---

delirious: *dazed and confused*
convulsions: *uncontrollable muscle spasms and movements*

A victim of ergotism (St. Anthony's Fire) appealing to St. Anthony for aid

Take Note

Doctors know a lot more about ergotism than they do about the previous two medical conditions discussed. But ergotism takes the #8 spot because the ergot fungus can be both good and bad for you.
• Have you ever eaten something that made you ill? What did you have to do to get better?

5   4   3   2   1

Jojo, a victim of congenital hypertrichosis, was a circus attraction in the early 1900s.

E HAIR

MEDICAL NAME: Congenital hypertrichosis (con-jen-it-al high-per-try-co-sis), also known as CH

CAUSE: It may be an inactive gene that has suddenly become active.

WHAT'S WRONG: Uncontrollable hair growth

Ever heard of congenital hypertrichosis (CH)? It is a genetic condition that causes excessive hair growth. CH might be one of the least life-threatening medical conditions on our list, but it is still very devastating.

From birth, thick dark hair grows uncontrollably all over the body, in all the regular places and in places where it shouldn't be. There's so much of it growing everywhere that eventually there's hair over almost every inch of the body. People with CH can end up with so much excess hair that they can have trouble breathing, eating, and even seeing properly.

In the past, people with CH had to face taunts like "wolfman" or "werewolf" or "ape man." They were forced either into hiding or into circuses. This doesn't happen anymore, but CH still remains a problem that has left even doctors baffled.

CH: EXCESSIVE HAIR

CAUSE

The unusual explosion of hair growth in CH is caused by a genetic defect — something that must be inherited from the parents. Some doctors believe that people with CH carry a mutated gene in their bodies that acts like a light switch. It turns on an ancient human trait that was switched off many years ago. How that works, we still don't know. But it makes perfect sense … you see, our ancestors were once covered with hair from head to foot — just like people with CH today.

SYMPTOMS

Hair really grows everywhere for people with CH. Some have hair covering over 90 percent of their bodies! Basically, where there's skin, there's hair. The only places with skin that are spared are the palms and soles. The excess hair is just like regular hair; there's nothing strange about it, just where it grows and how much of it there is.

mutated: *changed*

TREATMENT

Doctors are not entirely sure how the gene that causes CH mutated. They haven't yet been able to come up with a cure for CH. Without a cure, people with CH have to try to live with the disorder as best as they can. Some just live with it — they don't do anything to their hair. Others try to remove the hair by shaving, waxing, or bleaching it off. Unfortunately, the hair grows really fast, so it can take multiple shaves a day to stay bare.

If doctors discovered the gene that causes excessive hair growth, who else would benefit from the discovery, besides people with CH?

The Expert Says...

" This is probably a mutation of a gene that was a sleeping beauty. The mutation awakened a gene that had been put aside during evolution. "

— Dr. Jose M. Cantu, head of genetics, Mexican Institute for Social Security in Guadalajara

Jesus Aceves — one of over 20 people in the Aceves family with this condition

IN THE NEWS

You might be surprised by the attitudes revealed in these hair-raising newspaper headlines!

I'm Not Evil!

Hidden Lives: It's not Easy Being a Wolf Boy
The Sun, October 1, 2005

LONDON — A real-life "wolfman" reveals how he's had to fight prejudice due to his hairy condition. Jesus Aceves's face is his fortune … and can only find work in a circus as "Wolfboy" …

Real-Life Werewolves

ABC News

August 1, 2006 — We've all heard the werewolf legends: When the moon grows full, so goes the legend, a man is transformed into a beast — he grows hair, and acquires awesome powers. But what if it weren't the light of the moon but rather genetics that gave the werewolves of legend all that hair? …

Modern "Wolfmen" May Have Inherited Ancient Gene

The New York Times, May 31, 1995

NEW YORK — Casting a slender ray of light on the mysteries of both hair growth and the legend of the werewolf, scientists have discovered a gene that in its mutant form causes hair to sprout thickly and thoroughly across the face and upper body, covering the cheeks, forehead, nose, even the eyelids …

Portrait of a man with CH

Newspaper headlines are written to get your attention. Do you think these headlines are fair? Are they cruel? How could you write them in a kinder way?

Fur Better or Worse...

Daily Record, January 11, 2002

GLASGOW — Circus wolfman Larry Gomez — whose entire body is covered in black hair — married his teen love Nadine Lee yesterday. Larry, who suffers from the rare medical condition hypertrichosis, looked delighted as he and Nadine, 18, exchanged vows …

Hairy Girl Getting Best Treatment

The Bangkok Post, October 27, 2004

BANGKOK — Doctors at Siriraj Hospital are doing their best to help a four-year-old girl born with hair covering her face and other parts of her body. …

Quick Fact

There have only been about 50 known cases of CH since the Middle Ages.

Take Note

We ranked congenital hypertrichosis at #7, because people with CH experience a lot more problems in social life than people with the last three medical conditions.

• What are some problems that people with CH have to live with? What can be done to help them? In a different world, where less emphasis is placed on physical appearance, would CH still be considered "extraordinary"?

5   4   3   2   1

Elephantiasis of the legs

IS

MEDICAL NAME: Lymphatic filariasis (lim-fa-tic fill-ah-rye-ah-sis), also known as LF

CAUSE: Worms from infected mosquitoes

WHAT'S WRONG: Limbs swell up to elephant-like proportions and the immune system is damaged.

Elephantiasis is caused by parasites that enter the body through bites from infected mosquitoes. These mosquitoes carry the parasites as larvae in their mouths. So when the mosquitoes bite someone, they pass on the parasites. At first, victims of the disease have no clue they're carrying the parasites in their bodies. The parasitic worms hide in pockets of the lymphatic system called lymph nodes. Over time, once the worms have multiplied into the thousands and even millions, they short-circuit the system until it can't do its job anymore. Fluid collects and causes swelling in parts of the body. Not only that, the disease can turn the skin into what looks like the hide of an elephant. As if all this wasn't bad enough, the dreaded parasites can also cause serious permanent damage to the body's immune system.

parasites: *organisms that feed off your body*
larvae: *worm-like babies of insects that hatch from eggs*
lymphatic system: *system that runs throughout the body and directs fluid from body tissue to the bloodstream*

ELEPHANTIASIS

Health education class on lymphatic filariasis

CAUSE

The scientific name for elephantiasis, lymphatic filariasis (LF), gives us a clue as to its cause: filarial worms that attack the lymphatic system. These filarial worms are parasites. They use their victims as hosts, growing and reproducing until they've overloaded and destroyed their hosts' bodies.

? Experts say it's more important now than ever before to study and track diseases such as LF. Why? Think of increasing global travel and migrating human populations.

SYMPTOMS

Elephantiasis is a very painful disease. It causes a lot of swelling in different parts of the body and also turns the skin thick and dark, like the hide of an elephant.

Quick Fact

In tropical and subtropical areas where LF is well established, infection rates are going up. It now affects close to 200 million people in 80 countries. One of the main reasons behind the increasing number of victims has to do with the explosion of new but poorly planned cities. This has created unlimited breeding grounds for the mosquitoes that transmit LF.

TREATMENT

Doctors cannot simply punch a hole into the swelling and drain the excess fluid. That's because the fluid isn't sitting in a pocket of flesh, but rather inside body tissue. (It's like the difference between a water balloon and a wet sponge.) So what can doctors do? Recently, researchers came up with a new drug that can help kill the parasitic worms that cause LF. And others have discovered that cleaning affected areas with soap and water helps to keep the skin from blistering. Of course, the best treatment for LF is prevention — using bug spray, draining pools of standing water to destroy mosquitoes' breeding grounds, and sleeping with bed nets.

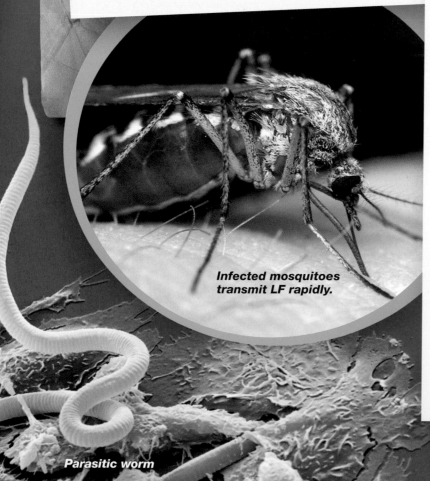

Infected mosquitoes transmit LF rapidly.

Parasitic worm

BEYOND THE LIMBS,
A DISEASE'S HIDDEN AGONY

A newspaper article from *The New York Times*
By Donald G. McNeil Jr., April 9, 2006

Antoinette St. Fab, 30, sells rice and oil in an outdoor Leogane market. Both her legs are swollen, but the left is enormous, almost a foot thick.

"In the past, I used to carry things like spaghetti and canned milk on my head and walk around selling them," she said. "But I can't do that anymore."

Because she now washes her legs frequently and smears antibiotic cream on them, she rarely has the fevers of infected ulcers anymore. But the pressure hurts, and she has trouble finding even flip-flops to wear. She tries to hide her legs under ankle-length skirts, but she must slit them very high to walk.

Her husband left her when he realized that her legs would not shrink, she said. As her new boyfriend, a handsome out-of-work carpenter, sold goods nearby, she said, "I don't know if he will leave me, too."

The other market women can be vicious. "I stepped on someone's foot by accident, and she said, 'Hey, yam leg, don't put your fat foot on me.' I told her: 'Oh, be quiet. God gave me this leg. Do you think that if I went to the store to buy a leg, this is the one I'd choose?' " …

ulcers: *breaks or sores on the skin*

Why do you think experts call LF "a disease of the poor"? How is this disease similar to ergotism at #8?

The Expert Says…

" People with elephantiasis seem to disappear. They often don't go outside because they are embarrassed. They may be ostracized by the community. They can't wear shoes, and so they rarely attend church or any social activities. "

— Pat Lammie, parasitologist, Centers for Disease Control and Prevention (CDC)

ostracized: *shunned*

Take Note

Elephantiasis comes in at #6 because its terrible effects are permanent and it can even affect the patient's family and community.
• Why might governments worry about a disease like LF?

5   4   3   2   1

CEP patient Jonathan Pierce (age 9) of Rossiter, Pennsylvania, tries on his "NASA suit" for the first time. The suit will help protect him from the sun.

L DARKNESS

JONATHAN PIERCE—ASSOCIATED PRESS, INDIANA GAZETTE

MEDICAL NAME: Congenital erythropoietic porphyria (e-rith-roh-poi-e-tic por-fear-e-ah), also known as CEP

CAUSE: A sudden interruption in the production of red blood cells

WHAT'S WRONG: Patients can burn up in the sun.

A mysterious blood condition may sound like the stuff of ancient vampire and werewolf legends, but it exists in our world! The highly unusual and rare disease is called congenital erythropoietic porphyria (CEP). People do not contract it — they are born with it.

People with CEP are super sensitive to sunlight from the second they're born. This means they can only go outside at night because even just a little sunlight can "burn" them terribly. CEP can also make teeth turn dark red so they look like fangs dipped in blood.

CEP: ETERNAL DARKNESS

CAUSE

When the body is producing red blood cells and something goes wrong, a backlog of "porphyrins" (por-fear-rins) starts building up in the body. With nowhere else to go, these porphyrins are just dumped into the skin. Unfortunately porphyrins are extremely sensitive to light.

SYMPTOMS

Even just a little bit of light can make porphyrins behave badly and cause symptoms of CEP. People with CEP have to be careful about avoiding sunlight, which can destroy their skin, leaving blisters the size of quarters. Constant blistering makes the skin more and more fragile over time — mouths, noses, and ears have been known to just wear away. People with CEP also find that their gums might recede, making their teeth look especially long. The excess porphyrins don't just sit in the skin either. They can find their way into teeth and urine, giving both an eerie purplish red color.

porphyrins: *compounds that help form red blood cells*
recede: *pull back*

Quick Fact

Many veterans of the Vietnam War returned with a milder form of this disease, because they had been exposed to the chemical Agent Orange.

The blistered hands of a CEP sufferer

Quick Fact

A weird twist this disease can take is that the body will grow more hair over time, to protect tender skin from the sun. In other words, people with CEP eventually have to deal with a form of hypertrichosis (#7 on our list!).

TREATMENT

The only way to cure this unusual disease is to get rid of the source of the problem: the blood! People with CEP will try blood transfusions and bone marrow transplants to remove the porphyrins that make them react so terribly to sunlight. Surprisingly, most people with CEP do survive into adulthood by staying out of the sun. In the future, doctors might move beyond replacing blood and go all the way to cells and genes to fix the problem!

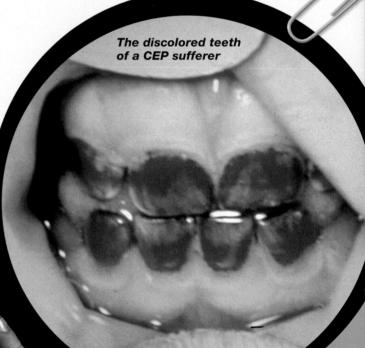

The discolored teeth of a CEP sufferer

The Expert Says...

" Without treatment ... congenital erythropoietic porphyria ... can be grotesque, ultimately exacting the kind of hideous disfigurement one might expect of the undead. "

— Dr. Nick Lane, University College, University of London

A TALE OF TWO BABIES
The Real-Life Stories of Baby Edwin and Baby Kasey

It was the best of times, it was the worst of times. This descriptive account follows the journey of two babies with CEP as doctors race to find out what their mysterious condition is.

When babies Edwin Rivera and Kasey Knauff came into the world, their parents must have promised to fill their lives with sunshine and happiness, just like every other parent would.

Both babies looked perfectly healthy at first, but things started going wrong shortly after.

Edwin and Kasey's doctors thought at first that they had jaundice (where the skin and whites of the eyes look like they've been stained yellow). So they were put under special lights as a form of therapy.

But the intense lights only made things worse …

"During the night the Rivera baby developed the weirdest rash I've ever seen … blisters all over his body." — Dr. Andy James, head of Newborn Intensive Care Unit

"She swelled three times her size. She turned red, blue, black and blue from head to toe. Nobody knew what was going on."
— Kurt Knauff, baby Kasey's father

Luckily for both Edwin and Kasey, the next doctors to jump in were dermatologists (who specialize in skin disorders). They took one look at the two babies and knew something was very wrong.

Both Edwin and Kasey's small bodies were terribly burned after going under the lights. The weird thing was, they weren't completely burned — their backs and other parts of their bodies that hadn't been exposed to the light were perfectly fine!

From there, just one more check would lead directly to the diagnosis no parent wants to hear.

When Edwin's doctors used a black light to look at his diaper in the dark, his urine glowed neon red. Kasey's doctors also saw that her urine was a strange reddish color.

This confirmed it: the two babies had CEP.

? Take a closer look at the process that doctors went through to diagnose Edwin and Kasey with CEP. Why do doctors need to go step-by-step to make diagnoses?

Quick Fact

Many historians believe that King George III of England had a form of porphyria. But they're not absolutely sure. Back then, even royal physicians weren't allowed to do extensive physical exams on the king, so their notes were simply based on what King George told them about his condition.

Take Note

CEP comes in at #5 on our list, because it causes shocking and terrible symptoms that make life very hard for patients. And unlike LF at #6, CEP cannot be prevented or treated with drugs.
• What would you have to change about your daily routine if you had CEP?

5 4 3 2 1

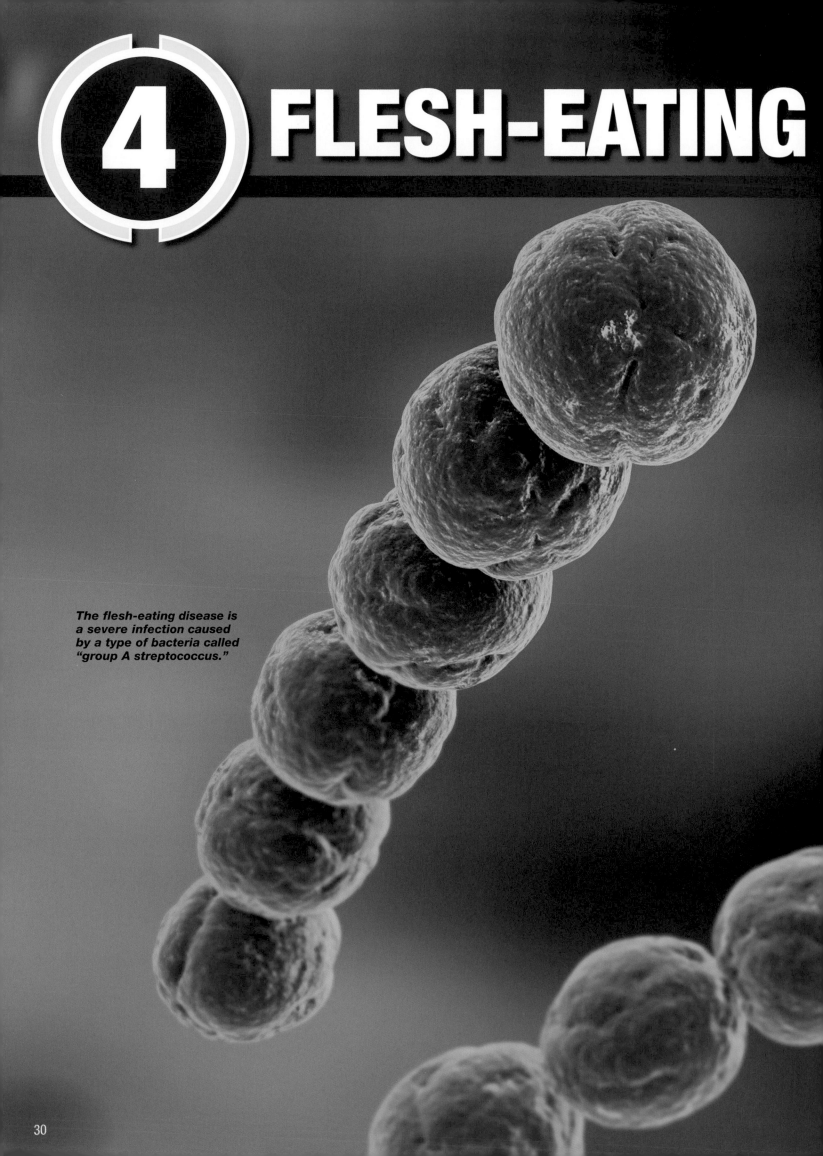

4 FLESH-EATING

The flesh-eating disease is a severe infection caused by a type of bacteria called "group A streptococcus."

DISEASE

MEDICAL NAME: Necrotizing fasciitis (neck-row-tie-zing fash-ee-eye-tis), also known as flesh-eating disease

CAUSE: A common type of bacteria that finds its way into blood or body tissue

WHAT'S WRONG: Infected body tissue can be destroyed within the first 24 hours.

The flesh-eating disease needs almost no introduction. It's as scary as it sounds.

Usually, when you're infected with nasty bacteria, your body is quite capable of healing itself — especially once you've got your hands on some antibiotics. However, the flesh-eating disease is no ordinary infection. Once you become infected, an inch of tissue gets destroyed every hour! Every flesh-eating infection is a race against time. In most cases, there's not much you can do besides having your infected tissue removed. Some patients may even have their infected limbs amputated to save their lives.

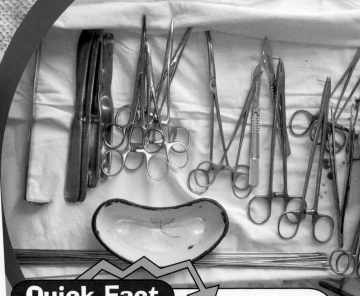

FLESH-EATING DISEASE

CAUSE

There's nothing unusual about the type of bacteria that causes the flesh-eating disease. In fact, it's the same type that causes ordinary strep throat in millions of children in North America every year! But if the bacteria find their way into blood or body tissue, that's when things can go terribly wrong, terribly fast. The invading bacteria release toxins, which shock the body into releasing infection-fighting antibodies. This response means well, but it's what ends up "eating" your flesh!

SYMPTOMS

The antibodies actually make tissues swell so badly that the oxygen supply gets cut off. Body tissue needs to breathe too, so if they don't get oxygen, they can die! This feels like a really bad bee sting at first, but then a purplish rash appears as tissues start to decompose. Within hours, the rash turns into large dark blisters filled with pus, because the flesh has basically begun to rot. Before long, the entire body goes into toxic shock, because it can no longer stop the toxin-releasing bacteria. This is so painful, most people will black out before they realize they have to go under the knife to carve off the rotting flesh.

toxins: *poisons*

Quick Fact

What a hoax! In 2000 and 2005, an e-mail circulated through the Web warning people to stay away from bananas because a batch that had entered the United States carried the flesh-eating bacteria! The U.S. Food and Drug Administration (FDA) and Centers for Disease Control and Prevention (CDC) later confirmed that it was just a nasty hoax.

What information here might explain why most people with the flesh-eating disease miss the chance to get early treatment?

TREATMENT

Getting medical help as soon as possible is crucial. Antibiotics can help stop the disease from spreading. But the only real way to get rid of the infection is to get rid of the infected tissue itself. In cases where the infection has gone too deep, doctors might have to carve right to the bone. That's not even the worst-case scenario. If the infection can't be contained or controlled, there's only one option: complete amputation.

9   8   7   6

A Survivor's STORY

What a close call! Here's a descriptive account about one woman's near-death experience with the flesh-eating disease ...

Ten years ago, a small cut in Catherine Mulvale's finger led to an infection of flesh-eating bacteria. Doctors gave her a 10 percent chance of living.

Mulvale went to bed one evening feeling fine. But the next morning, she woke up with flu-like symptoms and pain in her arm and back. In the next two days, she went to two clinics and her doctor's office, but nobody knew what was wrong.

Finally, seriously ill, she went to the emergency room of her local hospital where she was placed in intensive care before being transferred to a larger hospital. It was then that doctors told her husband to contact the family — they thought she might not make it.

Mulvale had to have eight surgeries on her right arm and shoulder before all the rotting flesh was removed and the disease halted. She doesn't remember much about her first few days in the hospital. But she recalled how painful it was when her open wounds had to be cleaned and disinfected.

Mulvale knows she was lucky to have survived. Now she works hard to warn others so they don't have to go through what she did. She says she can't stress enough how important it is to get an early diagnosis so that the right antibiotics can be given.

She also wants people to be responsible for their own care. "If you are afraid that medical people aren't acknowledging that something is really wrong with you, then go back again," Mulvale says. "Make sure you take notes on things like temperatures and symptoms.

"And always ask questions."

Lucien Bouchard, former premier of Quebec, a province in Canada, lost a leg to the flesh-eating disease in December 1994.

The Expert Says...

" It destroys tissue very quickly. It goes faster than antibiotics can kill the bug. "

— Hugh Pennington, microbiology specialist, University of Aberdeen

Take Note

The fast-acting aspect of the flesh-eating disease is one of the reasons why it comes in at #4 on our list. It doesn't just sit in your body, like CEP at #5 or elephantiasis at #6. And in terms of treatment, only a team of quick-thinking doctors and surgeons can help you.

• Besides forcing doctors to act quickly, what other difficulties does this disease present to the medical world? Think of the role that the patient has to play here.

5   4   3   2   1

SCID burst onto the scene in the 1970s with the story of David Vetter, the first documented "bubble boy." He lived with SCID for 12 years — surviving his childhood years in a plastic, germ-free bubble.

A BUBBLE

MEDICAL NAME: Severe combined immunodeficiency (e-mewn-o-dee-fish-en-see), also known as SCID

CAUSE: Mutated genes

WHAT'S WRONG: Being born with an immune system that doesn't work means every infection could be a patient's last.

Imagine what it would be like to spend your life in a bubble, completely separated from everything and everyone else in this world. What would you do if even the simplest things in life — like going outside to play or eating dinner with your family — were impossible?

Bubble boy condition, or severe combined immuno-deficiency (SCID), is yet another genetic disorder that can have a devastating effect on young patients. Not only does it destroy the immune system, it takes away your freedom and connection to the outside world.

SCID is more common than you may think — as many as one in 50,000 babies are born with it each year around the world. Some doctors think there may be more, but it's hard to tell — many babies born with SCID die before they are even diagnosed.

This disease may have a cute name, but it has unthinkable and fatal effects. It takes the #3 spot on our list of the 10 most extraordinary medical conditions.

SCID: LIFE IN A BUBBLE

CAUSE

Children born with SCID either have white blood cells that don't work properly, or their bodies destroy their white blood cells as soon as they're produced. Mutated genes inherited from the parents are to blame in both cases. Without healthy white blood cells to fight infections, the body's immune system is basically worthless.

SYMPTOMS

By taking away a working immune system, SCID leaves its victims with absolutely no protection against a common cold virus, a bacterial infection, or even athlete's foot fungus. It's like fighting a war with no weapons! Even the simplest of infections can, and usually do, spell disaster. Babies with SCID can also have trouble growing and gaining weight like healthy babies.

TREATMENT

As scary as SCID sounds, doctors do have an answer. Babies born with SCID can have a healthy immune system if they can get a bone marrow transplant within three months of birth. New blood-forming cells are introduced into the body to completely rebuild the immune system. But the average age at which babies are diagnosed with SCID is just over six months, well after the "window of opportunity" for this type of treatment. In this case, the next best thing is gene therapy — a new and experimental treatment that tries to fix the mutated gene that causes SCID.

? If you were the attending physician to a baby with SCID, would you recommend the experimental gene therapy treatment to his or her parents? Why or why not?

Quick Fact
Your immune system is actually a whole network of organs, blood cells, and tissue — everything must work together in order to protect your body against invaders.

The Expert Says...
"This once-fatal disease should be now seen as a pediatric emergency, a condition that needs immediate diagnosis and treatment."

— Dr. Rebecca Buckley, chief of Duke Children's Hospital's division of pediatric allergy and immunology

4

5

6

10   9   8   7   6

Bubble Boy Comes Home From Hospital

A newspaper article from the *Toronto Star*

By Elaine Carey, Health Reporter, June 3, 2006

Tiny Parker DesLauriers has taken his first baby step toward a new life, leaving a hospital isolation room and returning to his home …

Within a few short hours yesterday, he saw his parents' ecstatic smiles for the first time, felt their skin, breathed fresh air, and played in the room that's been waiting for him for more than three months.

With only a day's notice that Parker was being discharged from the Hospital for Sick Children, Tracy and Kevin DesLauriers scrambled to clean every surface in the house with Lysol wipes, rewash all his clothes, professionally clean the car, and assemble his stroller.

The 4¹/₂-month-old baby was born with a rare genetic disease called ADA-deficient severe combined immunodeficiency (SCID), commonly called boy-in-the-bubble disease, which quickly destroyed his immune system.

Without treatment, he would probably die before age 2.

He's thriving now because of the enzyme replacement therapy he started receiving a few weeks ago but that will only stave off infection for the next couple of years.

Parker's only real hope is an experimental gene therapy treatment in Italy that has been tried on just six children in the world with limited but hopeful success. He's been accepted in the clinical trial and, if he continues to thrive, the family hopes to leave for Italy in October. …

---

enzyme: *protein that speeds up chemical reactions in the body*

Quick Fact

It's hard to diagnose newborns with SCID because they look pretty healthy for the first few weeks after birth. Even bubble-boy babies start off healthy, protected by antibodies from the mother.

Take Note

There's no doubt it's unusual to have your own body fighting and eventually killing a part of itself, like in the flesh-eating disease at #4. But not having the ability to fight anything at all is even worse! That's why we feel SCID deserves the #3 spot on our list.
• What would you miss the most about your daily life if you had to be separated from the outside world?

Jimmy Livingston (Jake Gyllenhaal, left) is protected from germs in the 2001 movie Bubble Boy.

5   4   **3**   2   1

Roughly one in two million people worldwide are born with FOP.

WN BONES

MEDICAL NAME: Fibrodysplasia ossificans progressiva (fye-bro-dis-play-sha os-si-fi-cans pro-gress-e-va), also known as FOP

CAUSE: Mutant gene

WHAT'S WRONG: The body tries to grow a second skeleton!

"I saw a woman today who finally became hard as wood all over." When a doctor wrote this in 1692, he had just seen the grim death that a patient had suffered as a result of what would later be called fibrodysplasia ossificans progressiva (FOP). It's a close runner-up on our list of most extraordinary medical conditions because it's rare, it's deadly, and it simply defies logic and understanding.

FOP is a rare genetic disorder that causes the body to produce a whole new skeleton on top of the existing one! It does this gradually, by making new bone grow everywhere, even in places where it shouldn't grow. Over time, ribbons and lines and even whole layers of bone grow everywhere until the entire body is locked up in a solid mass of bone.

Read on to find out more about this unusual bone-growing disorder and see if you think it deserves to be #2 on our list.

FOP: OVERGROWN BONES

CAUSE

The key to FOP is a mutated gene. Normally, this gene sends out messages to certain proteins in the body to repair the skeleton with new bone. When it's mutated, it tells these proteins to "repair" other parts of the body with bone as well. Armed with this new message, the body reacts to everything from bumps to bruises, cuts to sprains, even the prick of a needle, by making new bone at the injured area.

SYMPTOMS

Babies born with FOP look fine except for two deformed big toes. After a few years though, the strange bone growth begins. First it starts at the neck and spine, then it moves down and out to the limbs, and finally it shows up in the jaw. Little by little, the soft tissues — such as muscles, tendons, and ligaments — that connect normal bones together turn into pieces of bone. Some people with FOP can't sit down, others can't stand up — it all depends on which parts of their bodies get more of the new bone sooner.

TREATMENT

Doctors only recently found the mutated gene that causes FOP, so they're still a long way from knowing how to fix it. For now, there are drugs that can help manage the symptoms (such as pain and swelling). Just removing the extra bone isn't an option — FOP patients who have tried to do this find to their horror that it only makes it worse; even more new bone grows back!

? Even when patients find out that surgery only makes the bone growth worse, some still decide to get excess bone carved off. Why do you think they would choose to do this?

An x-ray can show deformities.

Quick Fact

FOP is not immediately life threatening, but some patients do die young (usually in their 40s). Why? Either because their jaws freeze shut so they can't eat, or their new bone bends their bodies too much so they can't breathe.

10   9   8   7   6

THE Spread of FOP

1 A few soft reddish masses suddenly appear on the back of a patient's neck. The lumps don't hurt at first, until they become hard and stiff.

2 The patient begins to notice that it hurts to move either the upper shoulders or back. That's because underneath the skin, ribbons of new bone are spreading.

3 One day, out of nowhere, the patient discovers he can hardly raise his arm past the shoulders. Panicked, he goes to the hospital for surgery.

4 Surgeons find tiny pieces of bones crisscrossing one another. They carve it all off and send the patient home.

5 The surgery is a success — sort of. The patient can move again, but it doesn't last. Inside, new bone growth explodes out of nowhere. The arms, shoulders, and back lock into place.

6 A few years go by with no major changes. Then a silly little accident; maybe the patient trips and falls down. The next day, he can hardly get out of bed. A new spurt of bone growth has begun, this time on the hip. But it doesn't stop there …

7 The bone growth is out of control now, spreading from the hips to the legs. At first the patient can still get around with the help of a walker. In a few more years, he likely won't even be able to move his legs, never mind walk …

The Expert Says…

"It is the cruelest disease that I've encountered. It imprisons people. It's like a molecular terrorist attack."

— Dr. Frederick Kaplan, a leading expert on FOP

Take Note

FOP is our #2 most extraordinary medical condition. The symptoms that it causes are painful, uncontrollable, and simply impossible to grasp. It's a terrible disorder that traps patients and their doctors, because it cannot be prevented or cured at this point.

• How would the discovery of the gene that causes FOP help doctors battle osteoporosis, a condition that causes bones to break easily?

5   4   3   **2**   1

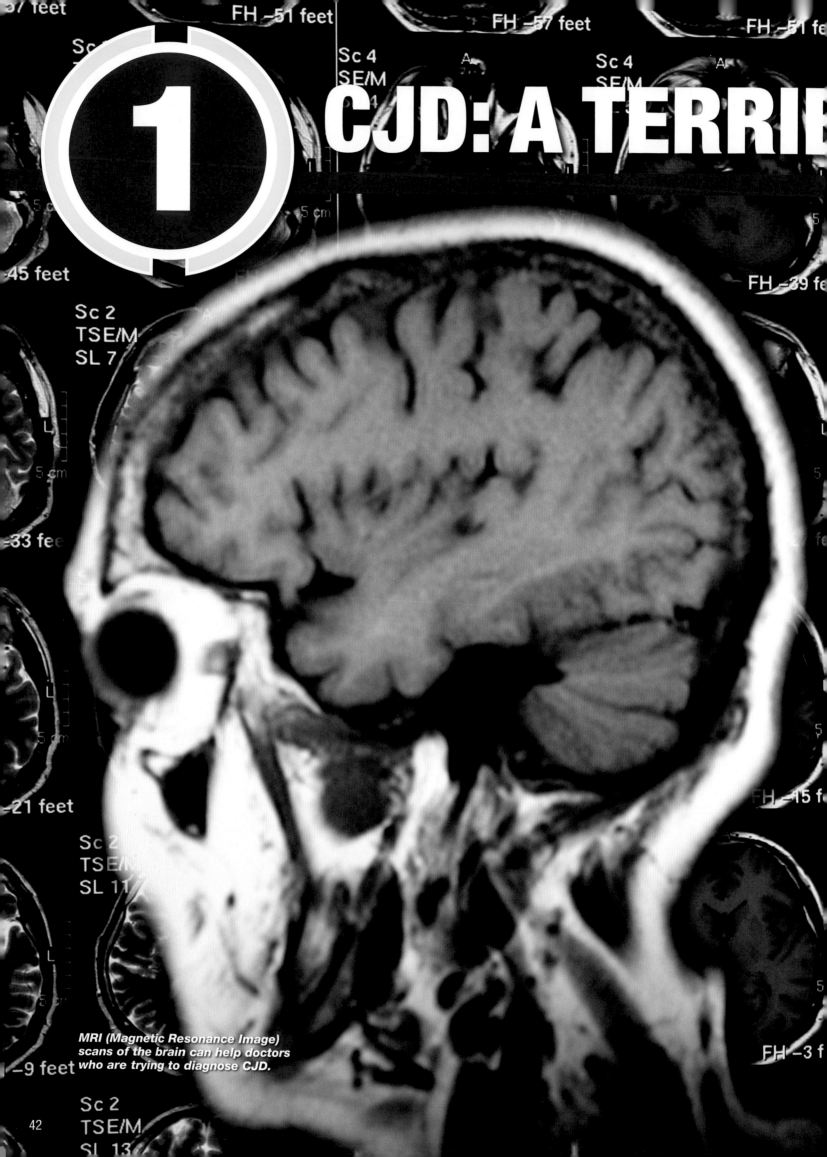

CJD: A TERRIE

MRI (Magnetic Resonance Image) scans of the brain can help doctors who are trying to diagnose CJD.

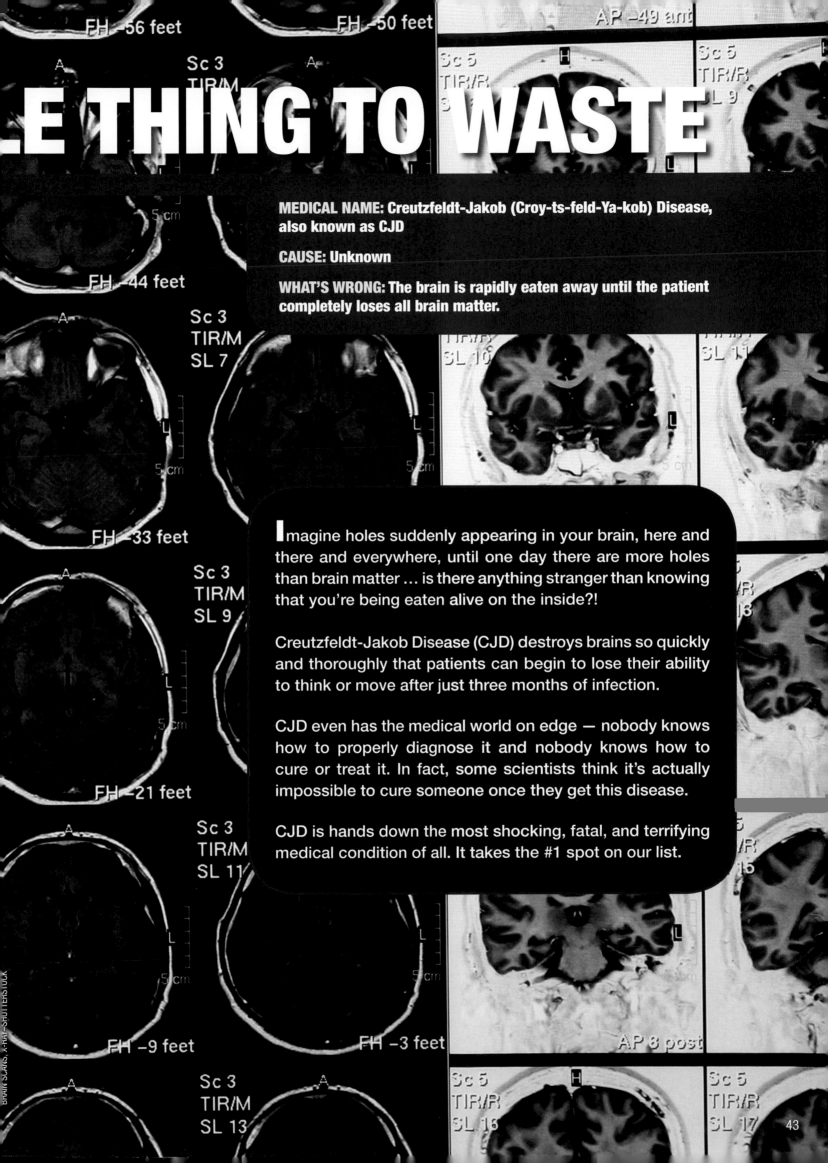

...E THING TO WASTE

MEDICAL NAME: Creutzfeldt-Jakob (Croy-ts-feld-Ya-kob) Disease, also known as CJD

CAUSE: Unknown

WHAT'S WRONG: The brain is rapidly eaten away until the patient completely loses all brain matter.

Imagine holes suddenly appearing in your brain, here and there and everywhere, until one day there are more holes than brain matter ... is there anything stranger than knowing that you're being eaten alive on the inside?!

Creutzfeldt-Jakob Disease (CJD) destroys brains so quickly and thoroughly that patients can begin to lose their ability to think or move after just three months of infection.

CJD even has the medical world on edge — nobody knows how to properly diagnose it and nobody knows how to cure or treat it. In fact, some scientists think it's actually impossible to cure someone once they get this disease.

CJD is hands down the most shocking, fatal, and terrifying medical condition of all. It takes the #1 spot on our list.

CJD: A TERRIBLE THING TO WASTE

CAUSE

Tiny deformed proteins called prions (pree-ons) are blamed for CJD, because scientists have seen them do one thing only: eat away at brains. What's odd is that in most cases, these prions become deformed spontaneously. In a small number of cases, people have contracted CJD because they inherited a gene that causes prions to develop. Another possible (but rare) way to get CJD is by infection with deformed prions after medical procedures. Last but not least, in recent years, many people have been infected with a form of CJD from eating tainted beef (from cows that had the "mad cow" version of CJD).

spontaneously: *as if coming out of nowhere*

SYMPTOMS

When the brain is slowly getting eaten away, what do you think could possibly happen? First the mind goes — the victim gets confused, moody, and forgetful. Then coordination goes — the person becomes clumsy and his or her arms or legs might jerk around awkwardly. This is all caused by the loss of brain cells in all parts of the brain, from areas that control thinking to areas that control muscles. As more brain tissue is eaten away, seeing and speaking become difficult. Eventually, CJD patients can't do much else except wait for death.

TREATMENT

So far, there's no cure or treatment for CJD because doctors still haven't figured out how to destroy prions. CJD is such an unusual disease that patients often don't get diagnosed with it (but then again, a diagnosis is no good when there's no cure!). In fact, taking out a piece of the brain for an autopsy (an examination after death) is often the only way to be sure someone had this disease.

How do you think doctors should deal with patients who show the beginning signs of CJD? If there's no cure, what should they do?

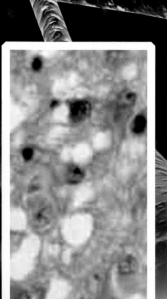

Normal brain   **CJD brain**

The Love of My Life is Gone - Not Forgotten

This personal account from Betty Wells describes her husband's battle with CJD.

My husband, Guy Wells, was a man of courage ...

After 1996, major changes came about in his health ... there were so many complications and symptoms that were similar to CJD, it was impossible to recognize it until he was in the final stages ...

The first time I knew something was really going on was October 13, 1998. After being admitted to the same hospital that he had gone to for many years, he became very confused. He thought I had taken him to a strange hospital in a town which had NO hospital. Even though he could not walk, for some unexplained reason he got out of bed and wandered down the hall to find me. The doctors ended up having to restrain him to keep him from hurting himself ...

We would talk about these episodes. Some things he could remember, but others he could not. It was like he was in another world at times ...

The hallucinations also began at that time. He saw so many things I could never list them all. But some of the things he saw were trains; he thought we were riding in an airplane. He saw children singing in a choir, a lady in a rocking chair, a creek running beside his bed ...

His attention span grew very short. It seemed that he could not remember day, time, and places and at times he did not remember persons ...

The Expert Says...

"[CJD is] a fascinating disorder ... and very much feared because it is one of the most invariably lethal cognitive disorders of the elderly, and sometimes can occur in the non-elderly."

— Dr. Lawrence S. Honig, Columbia University

Take Note

Everything about CJD baffles doctors. Since its cause remains a mystery, doctors still don't know how to treat, never mind cure, it. And because it destroys the brain so quickly and thoroughly, it's a truly terrifying disease. For all of these reasons, CJD takes the #1 spot on our list of extraordinary medical conditions.
• What do you think might have been the deciding factor(s) that pushed CJD to #1 instead of FOP?

5   4   3   2   1

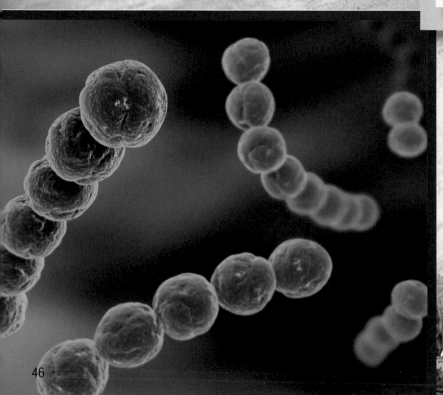

We Thought ...

Here are the criteria we used in ranking the 10 most extraordinary medical conditions.

The condition:
- Stumps doctors and scientists
- Is extremely rare
- Has an inexplicable cause
- Develops spontaneously
- Is hard to diagnose properly
- Causes astonishing or bizarre symptoms
- Leads to irreparable damage to the body
- Changes how the body reacts to regular things, such as the sun
- May be fatal
- Has no cure

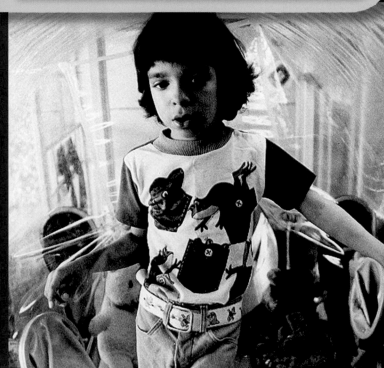

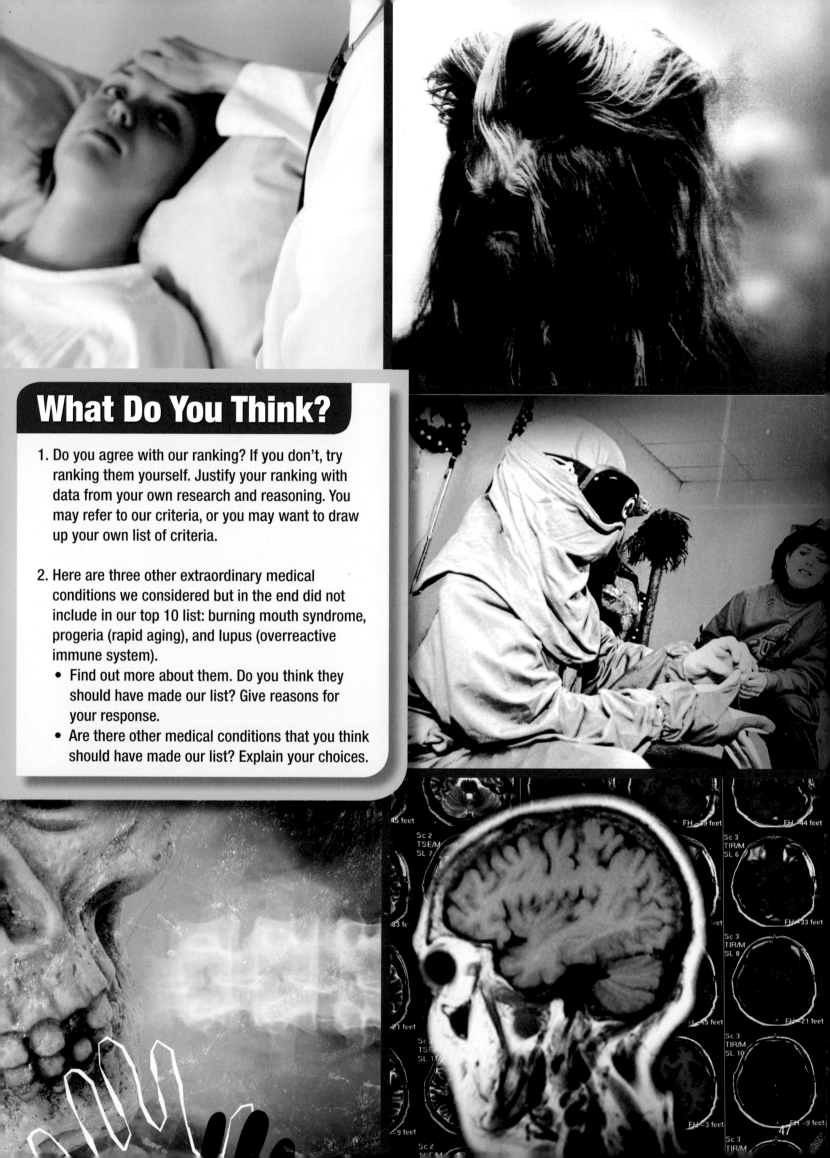

What Do You Think?

1. Do you agree with our ranking? If you don't, try ranking them yourself. Justify your ranking with data from your own research and reasoning. You may refer to our criteria, or you may want to draw up your own list of criteria.

2. Here are three other extraordinary medical conditions we considered but in the end did not include in our top 10 list: burning mouth syndrome, progeria (rapid aging), and lupus (overreactive immune system).
   • Find out more about them. Do you think they should have made our list? Give reasons for your response.
   • Are there other medical conditions that you think should have made our list? Explain your choices.

Index